Divorce

A Problem to Be Solved, Not a Battle to Be Fought

Karen Fagerstrom

with

**Milton Kalish,
A. Rodney Nurse
Nancy J. Ross
Peggy Thompson
Diana A. Wilde
Thomas W. Wolfrum**

BROOKWOOD PUBLISHING

Brookwood Publishing
P.O. Box 725
Orinda, CA 94563
Tel: 510-254-5598

Ordering Information:

Quantity sales. Special discounts are available on quantity purchases by corporations, associations, and others. For details, please contact Brookwood Publishing at the address above.

Orders for college textbook/course adoption use. Please contact Brookwood Publishing at the address above.

Printed in the United States of America.

Library of Congress Cataloging-in-Publication Data
Fagerstrom, Karen
    Divorce: A problem to be solved, not a battle to be fought / Karen
    Fagerstrom. Milton Kalish, A. Rodney Nurse, Nancy J. Ross, Peggy
    Thompson, Diana A. Wilde, and Thomas W. Wolfrum.
    1st ed. p. cm.
    Includes appendix.
    ISBN 0-9657519-4-5
    1. Divorce—United States.
    2. Children of Divorced Parents.
    3. Finance—Personal.
    4. Divorce—Psychological Aspects.
    346.73016 1997
    Library of Congress Catalog Card Number: 97-67346

Editing: PeopleSpeak
Illustrations: B. Benjamin
Interior Design: Joel Friedlander Publishing Services, San Rafael, CA
Cover Design: Lightbourne Images

Contents

Acknowledgments

The group of professionals who worked together to develop this book includes three psychologists, two social workers, a financial counselor and a divorce attorney. All of us have worked extensively with families who are divorcing. Our primary goal both in writing this book and in working together with clients is to coordinate our efforts to provide divorcing families with genuinely constructive methods of negotiating their way through the trying and significant family transitions that divorce brings.

I would like to thank the many families that each of us has had the opportunity to work with over the years. At the time of divorce, families often feel swept away by change and are terribly fearful of the unknown future. We admire the courage, hope and resilience of these families during difficult and uncertain times. We are grateful for all that they have shared with us and taught us about the demanding and challenging transition of divorce.

While I have had the privilege of and responsibility for writing the final text for this book, the ideas that are presented here stem from the collaborative efforts of many. I would like to briefly describe how this book has evolved and to acknowledge unique contributions of those who have participated in making the book happen.

The concept of working as a multi-disciplinary team, central to the Collaborative Divorce approach presented in this book, is attributable to the seminal thinking of Peggy Thompson and Rod Nurse. Over the past several years, Peggy and Rod have worked together tirelessly to develop and shape the fundamental ideas that have evolved into Collaborative Divorce. While Peggy and Rod consulted with many colleagues who shared their interests during the early formation of their ideas, Nancy Ross, L.C.S.W., and Diana Wilde-Neuman are gratefully acknowledged as having founding roles in the development of these ideas, and special thanks go to William Anderson, Esq., Faith Janson, Esq., Karlotta Bartholmew, Ph.D., and Grace Manning-Orenstein, M.F.C.C., whose contributions to these early discussions were substantial.

Those of us who have subsequently joined this work have added our own perspectives and expertise. Together we have further shaped, expanded and refined our collective ideas. We have grown to deeply appreciate the value of one another's contributions and to appreciate the perspective of each of the professional disciplines involved.

I would like to acknowledge those who have participated in the development of the content of this book for their significant contributions.

Financial counselor Diana Wilde-Neuman, whose idea it was that we put our thoughts together in the form of a book, has been the guiding voice in discussing the financial considerations facing divorcing couples. Her unique financial model of working with divorcing couples, developed with skill and vision, has been an invaluable contribution to our interdisciplinary approach.

Family law attorney Tom Wolfrum has provided a keen legal perspective and a compassionate understanding of the ways in which the legal process of divorce itself can become an additional burden or stress to couples who are divorcing.

Milton Kalish, L.C.S.W., has provided much-appreciated organizational and editing skills as well as artistic sensitivities and insights. His ability to help our work group attend to the process as well as the outcome of our work has been especially valuable to us as a group.

Nancy Ross, L.C.S.W., has contributed wisdom, thoughtfulness, and clinical expertise that reflects her compassionate commitment to and extensive background in working with divorcing couples. Her valuable perspective on the importance of communication skills is deeply appreciated both in her work with divorcing couples and in the gracious and constructive manner in which she has brought those skills to our work group.

Rod Nurse, Ph.D., who has worked with divorcing families in many settings and in numerous professional capacities (therapist, child custody evaluator, court-ordered dispute mediator, etc.) has contributed a rich appreciation for the systems-level dilemmas facing divorcing couples and an enduring dedication to the children who so often get caught in the middle of these dilemmas.

Peggy Thompson, Ph.D., has worked with passion, vision and remarkable perseverance in guiding the process of this collaborative book effort, always one step ahead, scouting the terrain to see what needed to be tackled next, what required attention, and what needed review. Peggy's capacity to juggle many details at once and her ability to persuasively enlist the enthusiasm and interest of others has kept our project moving ahead.

I would like to acknowledge the collaborative process of our work together as a team. This has been a true demonstration of both the demands and the rewards of collaborative effort. Just as the model of collaboration we present in this book requires effort and perseverance, so has our shared endeavor of developing this book. The results of these collaborative efforts include not only the appreciation of a final outcome but also great satisfaction with a meaningful process.

Thanks to the attorneys in Santa Clara and Contra Costa Counties for their interest in and commitment to collaborative law and an added note of recognition to Jonnie Herrting, Esq., for her review and comments on chapter 13.

A special thank you to Jean Petrick for her time, effort and good-natured resilience. Another very special thanks goes to all those involved in the production of this book, especially editor Sharon Goldinger, who was tireless in her effort to help us make this book user-friendly; Beatrice Benjamin for her illustrations; Joel Friedlander for his book design; and Shannon Bodie at Light-bourne Images for the cover design. Their commitment to excellence is appreciated.

We thank the following friends, relatives and colleagues for reading, reviewing, commenting on and supporting our work: David Glenn, M.D., Rick Riss, Ph.D., Janet Johnston, Ph.D., Grace Manning-Orenstein, M.F.C.C., Alice Wilde, Eric Nurse, and Daniel and Zachary Glenn.

Finally, we wish to express our deepest appreciation to our families, who have provided strong and enduring support and encouragement.

Karen Fagerstrom, Ph.D.
Berkeley, California

Introduction

Few words carry the emotional weight of "divorce." Divorce is not pleasant or easy, but it does not have to be emotionally gut-wrenching, financially destructive or damaging to your children. It is possible to go through the divorce process and come out "all in one piece," ready to go forward with your life and able to be an effective co-parent.

There may not be an alternative to divorce, but there is a better way: Collaborative Divorce—a new approach. In Collaborative Divorce, psychological, financial and legal experts coach and support you through the necessary problem solving and decision making for yourself and for your children.

Our many years of experience working with divorcing couples gives us a deep appreciation for the concerns and difficulties faced by divorcing couples. We have worked with hundreds of divorcing couples, providing psychological and financial counseling and legal representation. We have provided individual, group and family therapy and consultation to divorcing couples and their children. We have conducted court-ordered family evaluations and reviewed the evaluations of other professionals. We have served as "special masters" and as counselors under court order in high-conflict cases, and we have tried hundreds of divorce cases.

Our experience has taught us that

- Divorce is driven by emotions. It is not the work of the legal community to deal with people's emotions.

- In the current system, children are seen as property instead of people.

- By its very nature, the legal process is adversarial and narrowly focused. It can turn strong feelings and disagreements into ugly, entrenched fights.

Collaborative Divorce encompasses a broader view. In Collaborative Divorce

- Divorce is a problem to be solved, not a battle to be fought.

- The goal is to minimize the conflict of divorce.

- The premise is that coordinated problem solving benefits the family.

- Children are people and their needs and perspectives are important and must be recognized.

- An integrated professional team of divorce specialists provides skill and support to a family throughout the divorce process.

Who Is This Book For?

This book introduces a new approach to divorce to those individuals who want a better way: people contemplating divorce, mental health professionals and the judicial community.

Divorce affects all of us. When divorce leaves in its wake a damaged and fragmented family with parents who cannot cope and children who go uncared for, we all lose. When divorcing couples and their children get the support they need to make their way through difficult changes and lay the groundwork for a healthy future, we all benefit.

Collaborative Divorce will provide you with the steps necessary to accomplish an effective divorce that maintains the well-being of each member of your family. In an effective divorce, you become untangled emotionally as well as legally and financially. In such a divorce, your children are not caught in the middle of continued hostilities, and you are able to move forward and develop an independent and productive life.

Gender Issues, Couple Issues, and Clarification of Terms Used in This Book

In order to avoid sexism without the stylistic awkwardness of phrases such as "he and she," the genders of the personal pronouns have been alternated throughout the text wherever possible. The terms "husband" and "wife" are used because couples are married until their divorce is final. The term "couple" is considered plural to indicate that any marriage or divorce involves two unique individuals.

The word "collaborative" is fundamental to the understanding of our new concept. Collaborative, in general, refers to a team of people working together toward the same goal. Specifically in this book, it refers to the team of psychology, financial and legal experts (divorce counselors, financial counselors and attorneys) who coordinate their efforts with the divorcing couple to reach a settlement.

The term "adversarial" pertains to the traditional legal process—one side versus the other. In this instance, we are referring to husbands and wives and their attorneys working against each other, as opponents.

1 Coming Together and Coming Apart

Feelings Are Fundamental

People marry because of feelings.

People also divorce because of feelings.

But by the time a couple consider divorce, their lives have become much more complicated. During marriage, emotions, finances and property have intertwined. Divorce is the process of untangling what is intertwined.

Divorce: Battle to Be Fought or Problem to Be Solved?

Even when both partners want a divorce, they still experience loss and regret. They still face the work of making important decisions and coping with change. Usually by the time a couple decide to divorce, most of their good feelings for one another have dis-

appeared and have been replaced by a cloud of bad feelings.

Decisions on how to divide property, settle finances and establish custody arrangements require energy, attention and thought. But during divorce, people are often exhausted and preoccupied. They must not only manage to get themselves and their children through the emotionally tough times of divorce but also make critical decisions and plans for their own and their children's futures. This is like asking a quarterback to make a

game-winning pass playing
blindfolded in the rain.

It is easy to
understand

why divorcing couples have disagreements. But how
they handle those disagreements makes all the difference in the world. Stirred up with strong feelings about
divorcing and worries about the future, people often find
that their disagreements and differences can too easily
turn into battles, or worse yet, a full-scale war.

The currently available methods of divorcing don't provide people with the kind of help they need to solve the
many problems of divorce. Instead these methods often

draw people into arguments or make the arguments worse. Instead of untangling the knot, people end up in a tug of war. As each side pulls harder and harder, the knot tightens.

Once a divorce battle starts, it is very hard to stop. It's ugly, powerful and damaging. It's tremendously costly, both financially and emotionally. When divorce becomes an ongoing fight, it not only hurts the adults who are fighting but also can cause terrible damage to the children who are trying to survive in the divorce war zone.

A Better Way: Collaborative Divorce

Can you get a divorce without getting into a vicious tug of war?

Can you protect yourself and your family from the damage caused by disagreements that escalate unnecessarily?

Can you make constructive rather than destructive use of all of the important feelings you experience at the time of divorce?

Can you manage to make sound and thoughtful decisions about the future *and* deal with the tough challenges and changes of divorce at the same time?

The answer to all of these questions is yes. A noncombative way to end a marriage exists. Collaborative Divorce is a systematic, integrated process that helps divorcing couples manage conflict and stress, work through disagreements, solve divorce-related problems and make constructive plans for their own and their children's futures. Collaborative Divorce is a process that supports the resolution of problems while providing a way for people to protect themselves and their children financially and legally.

In Collaborative Divorce, a team of experts works together with a divorcing couple to help them develop thorough and thoughtful divorce settlements that take into account the needs and concerns of each family member. This team approach coordinates the efforts and expertise of family counselors, financial specialists and attorneys.

The Collaborative Divorce process features these positive aspects:

- Collaborative Divorce professionals share the belief that divorce is a problem to be solved, not a battle to be fought. They offer support, advice and assistance with the emotional, financial and legal aspects of divorce.

- The team works together to prevent unnecessary escalation of conflict.

- Each adult is provided with independent legal representation and individual divorce coaching and counseling.

- The counselors help divorcing individuals take an active role in determining how the process of the divorce is managed.

- The counseling process provides a safe place for disagreements to be heard and discussed.

- Children are given an opportunity to sort out their own feelings and bring to light questions and concerns about their changing family.

- Parents are given the help they need so they can provide coordinated, responsible parenting during and after divorce.

Our goal is to help maintain the emotional and financial health of the family while working toward achieving an effective divorce. We also aspire to help every member of the family develop constructive and realistic goals for post-divorce life.

2 Tying the Knot: How We Come Together in Marriage

"When I got married I was so in love I never thought it would end!"

The Emotional Contract

In saying "I do," couples exchange a spoken pledge to share the future with each other. But there is another kind of pledge or contract that is negotiated in marriage. This is an unspoken "emotional contract" about how each person expects the other to fulfill his or her fantasies, needs, expectations, hopes and dreams.

"I thought we were the perfect couple!"

The emotional contract worked out by each couple is unique. It involves the largely unstated understanding the couple have about what makes them "work" as a couple. Some emotional contracts are based on romance, some on camaraderie, some on agreeing to keep one's distance, some on agreeing to give and/or receive affection, some on competition, some on power, some on role expectations. The emotional contract is central to transforming two individuals into a "we."

The Financial Commitment

In saying "I do," couples begin life together as a financial "we" as well. Most often, couples marry with no idea about how they will handle monetary decisions together. Resolving this issue is something each couple does—more or less successfully—during marriage.

Over the course of married life, financial responsibilities and commitments increase, as do shared assets and debt. So the financial contract that couples make when they marry is a kind of leap of faith. The financial future of the couple is an unknown, but in marrying they agree to approach this unknown together.

The Legal Contract

The legal contract is simple and straightforward. Two individuals become one legal entity: partners in marriage. They sign a marriage certificate, which is witnessed by the maid of honor and the best man (or whoever is handy at the moment), and that's that. While each couple's emotional contract is implicit and unique, and future financial commitments remain unknown, the legal marriage contract is "one size fits all." Everyone signs an identical legal agreement.

Most couples don't give much thought to what they are signing when they marry. And that's why many divorcing couples become so bewildered when they decide to divorce. Two simple signatures bind them to a breathtaking array of legal commitments as a married couple. Divorcing couples find that getting out of a legal marriage contract is much more complicated than getting into one.

The Knot Gets More Complex

From day one, everything gets more complex in a marriage. The history a couple share together includes endless choices, decisions and shared ventures that involve the intertwining of feelings, finances and legal responsibilities.

Some of these choices and decisions are small-scale: What brand of toothpaste do we buy? Who balances the checkbook? Who decides when to buy a new car? How do plans for the holidays get made?

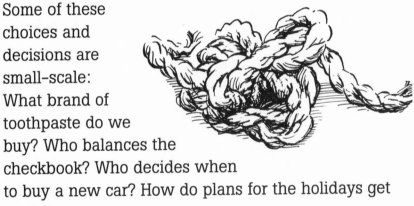

Other choices and decisions are more complex and significant: Where do we live? How are career conflicts handled? What if one of us invests poorly and loses the family nest egg? What if one spouse is so busy at work he or she misses out on the experience of parenting?

Of all the shared ventures in married life, none is more complex than becoming parents together. In choosing to become parents, couples make a long-term commitment to a life experience that is enriching, involving and demanding. Regardless of the direction a marriage takes, the relationships between children and their parents are lifelong.

3 Divorce: Untying the Knot

Divorce means untying the marital knot, which is held together with feelings. No matter what the cause of a divorce, the feelings evoked at this time are some of the most powerful and hardest to bear.

—

"I am on the verge of tears all the time."

—

"I think I am doing fine with my divorce, then I miss what people are saying to me at work. I guess my mind wanders."

—

Because every decision about the future brings up strong and traumatic feelings, it's hard for divorcing couples to think clearly about the important decisions at hand.

The decisions made at the time of divorce concern all aspects of shared life together. Everything—from the big-ticket items (like the house, the cars, the pensions) to the smallest possessions that have no monetary value but are priceless (like the coffee mugs your eight year old made at summer camp, the family dog, or the beautiful and beloved pieces of driftwood collected on a favorite family vacation)—is up for review.

—

"Jenny drew that picture for me for Father's Day. I let you hang it in your office, but it's still my picture. I want it back."

—

While property and financial decisions can be complicated and anxiety provoking, decisions about a couple's children are often the most difficult to face. Many times these decisions feel intertwined.

—

"The house means everything to me and the kids. I want the house. That's the least you can do after leaving the way you did!"

—

Emotional Issues

When faced with divorce, people have many different feelings: some people are devastated, some relieved, some very sad, some hopeful about the future, some resigned to it. Most people have more than one feeling about divorcing. Whether or not they want the divorce, it takes an emotional toll.

> *"I sat down to make my list of the items I wanted from the house and it brought back so many memories of our trips together. Everywhere I looked I saw things that made me sad."*

> *"I burned all my wedding pictures. They meant nothing anymore."*

> *"I think about when we had our first child and how close we were then. She's only three now. What went wrong so fast?"*

Divorce can feel like riding a roller coaster—so many ups and downs, quick jerky surprises, rapid twists and turns. Long anxious periods of anticipation are followed by fast, breathless plunges in new directions. Just like passengers on a roller coaster, divorcing individuals feel they have little control over what happens to them.

Some people fall apart under the weight of all their feelings. Others seem to carry on quite capably, only to break down unexpectedly. Still others work very hard at fending off or holding in their feelings.

"I thought I was handling our divorce well until the bank called to ask where my mortgage payment was, and I realized I'd forgotten to pay it. I never do things like that."

"I felt like I really needed a vacation to get away, but when I did, I couldn't relax. So I decided to come back and face the divorce."

Each person has to find his or her own way of handling the burden of so many different and difficult feelings.

Every divorce is unique, but there are some well-recognized themes about what can lead to divorce. Falling out of love, falling in love with someone else, growing apart, growing to dislike one another, becoming fearful of spousal abuse, being unable to forgive a hurt—these are just a few of the familiar themes.

Different feelings accompany different divorce situations. Feelings about a marriage that has run out of steam will differ from feelings about being left for another lover. The first might bring a cloud of sadness, loss, regret and relief; the second, a storm of hurt, anger, despair and desire for revenge.

Sometimes both partners want the divorce. More often, the divorce process begins with a substantial disagreement about whether or not divorce is the right decision.

"I didn't know she was so unhappy. I knew things weren't perfect, but when she announced she wanted a divorce, I couldn't believe it."

Just as each partner has unique feelings about divorce and unique ways of handling these feelings, the couple's ideas about how fast or how slow the divorce process should go may be at odds as well. If the wife wants a speedy divorce, she may accuse her husband of "dragging his feet." If she has a new relationship waiting in the wings, she may be eager to finalize the divorce. The husband who feels left behind may move at a snail's pace to punish his wife. Or perhaps he is hoping his spouse will have a change of heart, or he is simply too bereft to do anything at all for a time.

These differences—in feelings, in ways of handling feelings and in expectations about the time line for divorce— add friction to an already difficult situation. They make it even harder to communicate. Sometimes, divorcing partners can barely stand to be in the same room with each other.

Ann and Ray had been married eight years and had three children. They both worked, but she made more than he did and kept longer hours. Ray loved to stay home and tinker with woodworking projects. Ann was outgoing and loved to socialize; in fact, her work called for many social contacts and business dinners with associates. Ann found Ray dull but a good father. Ray thought Ann was a good mother but didn't spend enough time at home. However, they seemed to share parenting very well.

Ann had had one short affair four years ago but said she had been faithful since. When Ann announced that she wanted a divorce, Ray was shocked and emotionally devastated. He begged her to stay "for the children's sake." His depression became so bad he was unable to function. She stayed long enough to help him get the medication and counseling he needed so he could go back to work. Then Ann followed through with her decision and filed for divorce.

Ray became angry, sure Ann was leaving because there was another man. He told his lawyer that Ann had been a terrible mother and a cheating wife. When Ann heard these accusations from her attorney, she was devastated and angry and recalled how uninvolved Ray had been as a father: "He has been so totally immersed in his woodwork that he doesn't even know what the kids are doing. He just lets them watch television all the time."

Ann and Ray soon found it impossible to talk with each other because of their hurt and anger. They were furious with one another and went immediately to a custody evaluation, each asking for full custody of the children.

PARENTS' CONCERNS ABOUT THEIR CHILDREN

Concerns about children are among the most painful and wrenching parts of divorce. Divorce is an upsetting time for children, a time when they need extra sensitive attention. Parents must work doubly hard during divorce. Besides caring for their children during the stressful family changes, parents must also pay attention to the hard work of making agreements and arrangements for coordinating and parenting after the divorce.

"I can't bear the idea that he will have the children at Christmas. He never cared about Christmas. I did all the shopping and wrapping and baking. We always went to my parents' house for Christmas Eve. It's what the children have always known. They still believe in Santa Claus, and I want them to have that magic a few more years."

"My wife thinks that just because we always went to her brother's lake cottage in the summers, that's how it has to be forever. I'm not going to be locked into doing things her way; part of the reason we're getting divorced is I'm tired of her making all the decisions. I'm taking the kids backpacking next summer; I don't care what she says."

"Evan is supposed to have his bar mitzvah next year. How are we going to make it special for him when everything is such a mess?"

"I've invested five years in Girl Scouts with Jenny, and now her father is going to take that away from her. And from me too. I know he won't get Jenny to her scout meetings. He won't do anything for Jenny unless he's in charge of it. "

Almost always, kids don't want their parents to divorce, even if they know their parents have been fighting or are unhappy. Just as adults have a wide range of feelings to deal with during divorce, so do children.

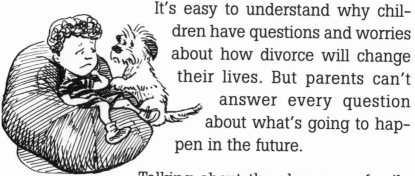

It's easy to understand why children have questions and worries about how divorce will change their lives. But parents can't answer every question about what's going to happen in the future.

Talking about the changes a family faces can be painful. Parents don't always know what to say or how to say it. They often feel so horrible about how divorce might hurt their children that they refuse to admit it has any impact at all, insisting everything is fine.

Determining custody arrangements and developing co-parenting plans is terribly difficult. The influences of anger, jealousy, hurt, betrayal and grief interfere with the capacity to make sound decisions about the children. Divorce can be such a big heartache to parents that they have a hard time keeping their children's needs in mind.

Even the most caring parents can lose sight of their children's needs in the midst of divorce.

"I hate coming home from work and not having my kids greet me. I feel so lonely. I'm terribly depressed, and I really need my kids."

"Whenever the kids ask for Daddy, I don't know if I am going to cry or tell them not to ask anymore since he doesn't really care about them. I know they miss him, but I can't stand to hear about it because all I can think about is what a jerk he is."

Divorcing parents find themselves in a terrible dilemma: How can they design a co-parenting plan with someone they have come to trust so little and hate so much? How can they coordinate the awesome responsibilities of parenting for years to come? How can each adult go on, untangled from the another, while still providing children with the best that each parent has to give? Untangling the emotional knot of marriage and at the same time deciding how to coordinate parenting takes every ounce of maturity each parent can muster.

Patti and Mike, a young couple married only four years, had a ten-month-old child. They were in the crisis of divorce. One night after the baby was asleep, they began to discuss the many decisions facing them. Their discussion turned into a huge and horrible blow up, and they each stormed out of the house. Mike headed to a friend's house; Patti decided to cool off at a late night movie.

They were both gone for over an hour before they each realized they'd left the baby home asleep. As they rushed home, they were shocked and sick with worry. It was absolutely inconceivable to either of them that this could have happened.

Financial Issues

Divorce can put a strain on any family's finances. The additional expenses of supporting two households can be overwhelming. While most people do worry about money when they are divorcing, few anticipate the full financial impact on the family.

When a couple divorces, they must undertake the difficult job of assessing what they have and how to split it up between them. What's owned and what's owed must be identified and then divided.

"I don't know anything about our finances. He always took care of all of that. He gave me house money and he took care of everything else. I have no clue what we really have."

Sometimes people are uncertain about their family's financial situation. One spouse may have been the exclusive money manager in the marriage, leaving the other feeling disadvantaged and uninformed. One person may be very savvy about some aspects of the family finances yet know nothing about other areas.

The financial history of the marriage can be so complex that it requires a lot of backtracking to determine the facts. Additionally, worry about the future makes it hard to make clear decisions about the financial aspects of divorce; the decisions get all tangled up with feelings.

"All he cares about is fixing up his cars and impressing his girlfriend. He doesn't care about his children and what they need."

"She's going to take me to the cleaners if I don't get a good lawyer."

"I told my son to tell his mom to stop spending so much money."

"He doesn't care if I end up a bag lady."

Slicing up the financial pie in a way that supports two separate post-divorce households is a sobering task.

For the short term, temporary budgets need to be agreed upon.

In the long term, untangling the financial ties that bind will include dividing up shared property and determining child and spousal support.

There is no surefire financial formula available that provides the "right" answer because each family has a unique set of circumstances. It takes time, thought and careful attention to untangle the family finances and constructively plan for the future.

Legal Issues

People getting a divorce need to know their legal rights. For most of us, reading the law is like reading a foreign language: confusing and frustrating. How can you make the best decisions if you are confused or uninformed about your rights?

Bombarded with stories about the divorces of the rich and famous and the newsmaking tragedies that occasionally result from divorce, people who are faced with divorce are understandably worried about their legal positions and how their divorce will be resolved. They are constantly asking themselves questions such as, How will our property be divided? What can I expect in terms of giving or receiving child or spousal support? What are our options for child custody? How can I make my way through all the legal aspects of divorce if I am unfamiliar with them? Is it best to get a lawyer or should

I try to do it myself? Should I agree to mediation or will that leave me in a position of having no legal advocate?

"Are we going to have to sell the house?"

"I'm worried that she'll automatically get the kids full time because she's the mother. I've been as involved as she's been every step of the way!"

"Our vacation condo was a gift from my parents. Does she get half of it now that we're divorcing?"

Although attorneys are the source of expert legal advice, people who are divorcing worry about going to attorneys for help. For those who do not want to divorce, putting off seeing an attorney is a way of postponing the inevitable; yet these people may end up feeling more victimized if they find they have no one who can represent them. People who are divorcing are often anxious about being able to understand the law and how it applies to them. They are also anxious that an attorney may not understand their situation or that they will not feel able to tell the whole story to a stranger.

"When I went to the lawyer he made the process sound so complicated that I felt I'd better turn everything over to him. I was so nervous I didn't understand anything he said."

People worry that involving an attorney will inflame tensions between a husband and a wife. If one person sees an attorney, the other may perceive it as an act of aggression, anticipating that the attorney will behave aggressively.

———

"She's gotten herself a big-name lawyer with a reputation for being a real killer in the courtroom. Well, I'm not going to wait around to get steam-rolled; she's in for a fight!"

———

"We went to court and the judge gave us an hour and a half to decide my life. I'm furious and completely broke!"

———

What if a legal battle develops? What if the case goes to court? People who are divorcing worry about how they will be able to agree on division of property, support and custody without ending up in a fight that goes to court. Everyone has heard stories about the entrenched bitterness that results from court battles in which legal experts "duke it out" on behalf of a divorcing couple until everyone is wrung out, miserable and financially depleted. Getting through the legal hoops of divorce and avoiding this kind of horror story is what most divorcing couples hope to do.

Getting through the legal hoops requires knowing what they are—that is, becoming informed—and carefully considering the range of choices available (traditional attorney, mediation, or do-it-yourself). Fully understanding the legal aspects of property division, support and child custody can be difficult in the midst of dealing with all the pressures and feelings that come with divorce.

———

"It cost me $5,000 just to straighten out our assets and debts with my attorney. Then my wife's attorney had to do the same thing and it cost even more. This is never going to end!"

———

"I've heard that you should ask for sole custody right off the bat, even if that's not what you really want."

———

"I don't understand if I should be asking for child support or spousal support."

———

Thinking through the short- and long-term impact of possible options is also tough. When feelings are running high and divorcing individuals are worried about what they can get or keep or how they can get justice for being wronged, considering anything but the strong feelings of the moment can be difficult.

The law concerns people's rights. However, in the words of Justice Potter Stewart, "There is a difference between what you have a right to do and what is right to do." When divorcing individuals become focused on their rights at the expense of what's right for the family, they run the risk of losing sight of the big picture for their children and for the future.

Untangling the legal knot of divorce requires the ability to consider the law and the rights of every person involved. The important decisions that must be made about division of property, support and custody take thought, courage and maturity. The passions of the moment make thoughtful decision making seem nearly impossible at times. Nevertheless, the divorcing couple are faced with making some of the most significant legal decisions of their lives.

This Is Hard Work

Getting divorced is hard work. No two divorces are identical, but all divorces do have this in common: patience, energy and effort are required in untangling what has become intertwined in the marriage.

4 Available Solutions: How We Commonly "Do" Divorce

The job of divorcing requires untangling the emotional, financial and legal knot that has developed over the history of the marriage. Cutting the legal ties alone does not do the job of untying the whole knot.

The common pathways by which people divorce usually deal with only one aspect of a divorce:

- You can take your chances at doing your own divorce and hope you don't run into difficulty.

- You can agree to go to a mediator and let him or her help you negotiate property and custody arrangements.

- You can each get separate attorneys and let them take charge.

- And if you can't reach settlement, you can turn your divorce over to the court and put the decisions in the judge's hands.

Sometimes these methods work, but they don't help you manage the overwhelming stresses of divorce. They may help you get the necessary paperwork completed, but they do not help you think clearly as you're trying to make important decisions about your future. In fact, often these methods are used in a way that escalates disagreements and differences. In such cases, divorce winds up as a battle to be fought instead of a problem to be solved.

What Fuels the Fire?

What causes a divorce to go out of control? What makes disagreements escalate?

Disputes become bitter fights when

- the bad feelings the divorcing couple have about one another increase to such a level that nothing but destructive interactions occur;

- outside influences such as friends, family, attorneys and therapists fuel the flames;

- systems that are in place to help people through divorce contribute to the problem.

EMOTIONAL TINDER

During the time of divorce there are many sources of stress and bad feelings. They pile up like tinder. Divorcing couples find themselves in a situation of "high fire danger." If the tinder ignites, the result can be a truly awesome bonfire of bad feelings.

"I feel terrible; I am so unhappy in this marriage. I just want out, but I feel guilty about the children. Their dad is a nice person, but I don't love him anymore."

"I never do anything right. This marriage is a disaster."

"When he told me he was leaving, I felt like I'd been hit in the face."

"I feel like this is all a bad dream. I walk through the days in a fog. I keep thinking she loves me and she'll come back."

"I'm barely keeping my head above water. Between work, the kids, the house and the hassle of trying to figure out how to get by on a shoestring, I never get to bed before midnight. I'm really burned out."

What follows is a list of some potentially dangerous emotional tinder:

guilt
outrage and fury
shame
feelings of abandonment
hurt and anger about being left
feelings of rejection
feelings of failure
loss of self-esteem
worry about the future
worry about the children
worry about finances
desire to escape
sense that one's life is a failure

depression

sense of unreality

bewilderment

fatigue

sense of carrying the whole load

estrangement from family and
  friends

loss of emotional support from
  spouse

shock

feelings of being traumatized

disbelief and denial

financial insecurities

This is only a partial list.

———

"Whenever it's time to write her a check, I call my lawyer instead. It's the money that makes me so mad! I'd rather give it to the lawyer."

———

"She's not getting another penny of mine! She'll take fancy vacations with her boyfriend over my dead body!"

———

"He has no right to even see the kids after what he's done."

———

"I want to get him where it hurts. He has taken my whole life. I want a lawyer who'll make him pay."

———

Each divorce is unique; the various feelings the wife has will not necessarily be the same or occur at the same time as those of the husband. She may have more emotional struggles than he has, for example. But during any divorce, some of the troubles listed above are bound to be present.

Sometimes Getting "Help" Makes Things Worse

As people try to find their way through divorce, they look for help from attorneys, mediators, psychotherapists, friends, family and co-workers. However, sometimes these people make matters worse. How can this be?

GETTING HELP FROM FRIENDS, FAMILY AND CO-WORKERS

The problem is that there are usually two distinctly different versions—his and hers—of what has gone wrong with the marriage and why a divorce is occurring. Each spouse tells a compelling story about what has led to the divorce. But at such a stressful time, each may have trouble recognizing and respecting the other's point of view.

To make matters worse, when the couple describe their situation to others—friends, family and attorneys, for example—they paint vastly different pictures of what's happening. People who hear the wife's story get "her" version, while the husband tells a very different tale, "his" version. Neither story is entirely right, but neither is entirely wrong. They simply reflect the different perspectives the couple hold and the differing experiences they have. The "we" of marriage is replaced by the "his" versus "hers" of divorce.

In describing the divorce story to others, each person is usually looking for understanding and support for his or her point of view. The competing versions of the story begin to gather separate followings. The wife recruits her group of supporters and the husband recruits his. In an attempt to offer support and understanding, family, friends, co-workers, therapists and others view the situation from only one perspective—that of the storyteller. The result is that, while these supporters may have a very keen appreciation of one point of view, by no means do they have an understanding of the whole picture.

Divorcing couples need to reach out and find support from those around them; however, the desire to draw people in to take sides against the other spouse can result in increased tension and bad feelings.

Another problem stems from the fact that nearly everyone has stories about divorce. The advice people offer may be based on their experiences and biases and not be pertinent to the divorcing couple's circumstances.

Advice from friends and relatives can also cause a terrible problem if it is given within earshot of the children. Children are like sponges soaking up the tone and the gossip of bitter conversations that they are not meant to, but do, overhear.

> Molly, a talkative and inquisitive five-year-old, came in to talk to her therapist. They were reading the *Dinosaur's Divorce* book together when Molly looked at her therapist and said knowingly, "My mommy is really mad at my dad. I heard her talking on the telephone to Grandma. Is Mommy really going to kill Daddy?"

GETTING HELP FROM MENTAL HEALTH PROFESSIONALS

Many people undergoing divorce seek help from psychotherapists and counselors. Often, the decision to divorce is reached in consultation with a counselor. At a time of high stress, many people reach out for support and for an opportunity to think through the important life events facing them. The help provided at such a time can be invaluable.

However, many counselors and therapists have had little or no training in helping divorcing families. They may not know the impact of their advice. When counselors meet with only one member of a divorcing family, the whole story of what's happening in the family and what's at stake is not known to them.

> *"My therapist told me not to talk to my wife about anything related to our divorce. But how can we resolve anything if we don't talk?"*

Finding support during a time of high stress can be comforting, but it may not be helpful if it edges people toward taking adversarial positions about divorce-related issues. Just as relatives and friends can add fuel to the fire, so can therapists. They can get drawn into the divorce fight and find they are taking sides in a way that causes the divorce to heat up even further. Counselors and psychotherapists can unwittingly make matters worse if, in their enthusiasm to support their clients, they encourage their clients to take strident or combative stands.

> *"My counselor said that I'm in the right and that I need to stand up and fight for myself. So I got the toughest lawyer I could find."*

GETTING LEGAL HELP

Lawyers are experts at the law. In divorce, they help their clients understand their legal rights and options, offer advice on possible outcomes, and help with the maze of paperwork that divorce entails.

However, representing the interests of one spouse against the other can fuel the flames of the dispute instead of solve problems. When lawyers go to battle against one another on behalf of their clients, disagreements can reach monstrous proportions. A fight between lawyers consumes huge amounts of time and money. In such cases, the embers of bad feelings quickly become a bonfire. Whoever gets in the way gets scorched. As a result, the lawyers may have waged a fabulous and powerful legal campaign, but the divorcing couple end up financially drained and entrenched in bitterness and anger.

"Your attorney told mine that I wasn't a good mother because I fell asleep in the afternoon when the kids were watching television. I work nights, for crying out loud. Of course I'm going to need to rest during the day. The kids aren't babies, they can be on their own while I'm napping. Who do you think you are, bad-mouthing me to your lawyer?"

Once a bonfire of such intensity gets built up, getting it under control is terribly difficult. If children are involved, the escalation of fighting between the couple may be so great that the job of providing necessary and appropriate care for the children becomes nearly impossible.

The emotional cost of such a bonfire of hostility is terrible to witness. And the financial cost lays waste to the family's savings. In the heat of the moment, a divorcing couple have trouble realizing it is the children's college education or the possibility of a comfortable retirement that's going up in smoke as the divorce process gets more and more legally embroiled.

An adversarial legal battle leaves the post-divorce family impoverished, drained and beset with lingering bad feelings.

In the worst of cases, one fight leads to another until finally the divorce war takes over and becomes the major theme in a family's life. This is a tragedy for everyone involved.

5 Current "Solutions" Add to the Problem

Problems in the System Add Fuel to the Fire

Divorce heats up when bad feelings build and when others get involved in the disputes and make them bigger. Yet another source of fuel for the fire is the ineffectiveness of the very systems that are supposed to help. When these systems fail to help, or make matters worse, people feel angry, victimized, lost and betrayed.

Ending a marriage is painful, but added to that pain are the awful speculations and worrisome unknowns that accompany the process of getting a divorce:

- People worry that they will be terribly misunderstood by those representing them.

- People are overwhelmed by the complexity of divorce and feel unsure about what options exist.

- They worry that when they turn to experts for help they will lose control over their own lives and give up their right to decide their future.

- They worry that if they don't get help and try to do their own divorce, they'll do something wrong.

- They worry they will not be able to hold their own in divorce mediation and will agree to terms before they understand them.

"We went to a mediator because I was afraid I would get stuck with the fees for both attorneys in a legal battle. Sometimes I felt the mediator was on my side, but every time she smiled at my ex, I felt afraid that she'd favor her. I felt trapped."

- They worry that the attorneys will be more interested in matching wits with each other than in really understanding a couple's true concerns and interests.

- They worry that what really matters will get overlooked.

- They worry that in the legal system, disagreements get resolved in a win–lose way; someone is going to win and someone is going to lose.

- They worry that small disagreements will turn into full-blown battles.

- They worry about losing everything financially in the process of divorce.

- They worry that the overflowing and overwhelmed legal system will not be able to really consider their personal and private life situation.

- They worry that ultimately, the system, overworked as it is, won't hear their story or care about it.

What's Wrong with the Way We "Do" Divorce?

Divorce is primarily viewed as a legal event, but first and foremost, it is an emotional event. The legal system treats divorce as if it were only a matter of reasonable men and women and their attorneys rationally arguing different points of view. It accounts for only one part of a complex problem, but it misses what's most important: the fact that divorce signifies a highly emotional major life change that affects nearly every single aspect of a person's life.

The law holds no answers for many of the truly fundamental dilemmas of divorce. The legal system handles the legal part of divorce, but in not recognizing divorce for what it is—an important emotional event—the solutions the system comes up with are at best partial. Some of the questions that divorce raises about managing the present and planning for the future cannot be answered by the law. They are practical questions that find their answers in the personal and individual choices of a family.

The legal system is notoriously adversarial. If a problem is tough, the ultimate legal solution is to get tough in court. However, getting tough in court has very little to do with truly solving the real and long-lasting problems of divorce. The legal system has no way to contain, much less extinguish, the emotional fires that often occur in a divorce. It's not the job of attorneys to take care of the emotional consequences that accompany divorce. But the current system provides no way to help people manage and understand their feelings. Instead, the adversarial process can make matters worse.

In court, it comes down to one story against another, with the understanding that in the final outcome, someone will be the winner and someone will be the loser. The reality is, everyone loses.

The courts are incredibly overloaded and understaffed. The courts are jammed with divorce cases that have gotten out of hand. They are not equipped to handle all the problems divorce brings. Once a hotly contested case gets to court, the court has to decide how to deal with it. Like a hot potato, the situation gets passed back and forth while last-ditch efforts are made to cool it down. No one wants to touch it. When the case finally gets to the family court judge, the judge may have only fifteen to twenty minutes to consider the entire divorce case.

In the current system, children become property instead of people. How a couple's divorce affects their children is a critical part of the process for any divorcing family. Yet in the current system, the needs of the children are barely heard. Parents get caught up in fights over the children, and what is best for the children is forgotten.

Children get lost in the legal shuffle. Attorneys are not child welfare specialists, so how can they advise divorcing people about their children? If decisions involving the children are brought to the attention of the courts, the issues often are taken up in a tone of adversarial debate instead of thoughtful deliberation.

There is no coordination of legal, financial and emotional help. At the very least, this means all the pieces of the puzzle don't end up on the table. Worse yet, sometimes the advice of one professional is the opposite of the advice of another, making the picture even more confusing.

Consider three blind men who each take hold of one part of an elephant and try to communicate with one another about the creature. They can't agree on what they have encountered.

The first blind man takes hold of the trunk of the elephant and concludes that he is wrestling with a snake. The second blind man grabs onto the tail and decides that he has hold of a rope. The third blind man touches the elephant's leg and decides he has embraced a tree trunk. All three argue about who is correct, who is accurate in his perceptions.

Are they all holding onto the same elephant? Yes. Do they understand the full and true nature of the creature? Well, they each may know one part very well, but working in the dark, it is very hard for them to talk about it together in a meaningful way.

The various professionals involved in helping people during divorce are very much like these blind men. The lawyers think of divorce as only a legal process, the financial advisors regard it as a monetary puzzle and the

counselors consider it a challenging emotional dilemma. Each is responsible for his or her area of expertise in the divorce. Each has a unique perspective about what's involved in divorce and what is most important to consider. Guided by different priorities, each addresses only a part of the whole.

The result is frustration, miscommunication and misunderstanding. Efforts are at cross-purposes, so time and money are wasted. A meaningful understanding of the family's situation is never achieved.

6 From Problems to Solutions

Through years of working with divorcing couples, we have learned about the pain of divorce. We know what people are confronted with when they go through a divorce. While each story is unique, every divorce has challenging emotional, financial and legal aspects. We have described these challenges in the first half of this book.

It is not just because the decision to divorce is such a huge emotional event that makes it so difficult. It's doubly challenging when the process of getting a divorce turns into a frustrating, confusing and combative nightmare.

While there is no way to make it easy or painless, we believe there are ways to make divorce less difficult and less painful.

We believe that in order to solve the problems of divorce

- first, you need to know what the problems are and where they stem from;

- next, you need to know what helps solve the problems and what makes them worse;

- then, you need to make sure that what really helps is made available to the people who need it.

In creating a new approach to divorce, we have worked together as therapists, lawyers and financial counselors to identify what we know to be helpful to couples as well as what we know to be unhelpful or harmful.

We are committed to addressing the problems of divorce and the problems of the system so that divorcing couples can get "help" that really helps.

In the second part of this book we share our system for positive change. We want to share our ideas with people who are going through divorce, with the general public and with professionals who work with divorcing families.

Divorce touches all of us, either directly or indirectly. Decreasing the damage divorce causes benefits everyone.

Change Is Needed

Our message to the general public is an invitation to consider the need for better ways of handling the difficult problems of divorce. We invite the public to think about divorce and the terrible toll it takes on so many families in our society. When divorcing families don't get the help they need, everyone in the family suffers—the effect even extends out to others in the community and into the future as well.

We want divorcing couples to begin to think of divorce as a process of problem solving. We hope they can approach the problems of divorce with a new and more constructive perspective and ask professionals to help them by working in the collaborative ways we describe here.

We are suggesting that the professionals who help people during divorce

- develop a perspective of working toward divorce solutions that values and provides for the well-being of the whole family;

- communicate with one another and work collaboratively to help the family arrive at solutions to its problems.

Our approach is the product of the shared thinking of a group of therapists, lawyers and financial counselors. We present our ideas to our colleagues in these professions and ask them to join us in working toward the development of integrated and effective methods of helping people through divorce.

7 Getting Help: Collaborative Divorce

Divorce Is an Emotional Event

We know that divorce is first and foremost an important emotional event. People want to make it through divorce intact and unscathed.

For some people going through divorce, powerful feelings sweep through like hurricane winds. For others, divorce is like a heavy gray cloud cover, difficult but manageable. No matter whether people are desperately trying to cope or simply trying to minimize the pain, divorce is a situation that stirs up feelings that are difficult to handle.

Collaborative Divorce helps people come to grips with the strong feelings that surface during divorce. Managing these feelings makes it possible to make decisions wisely and effectively.

Solutions Are Not "One Size Fits All"

Just as every couple is unique, so is every divorce. A "one-size-fits-all" perspective or set of solutions will not be effective or realistic. There are no cookie-cutter answers to the problems of divorce. Getting the legal documents filled out and processed correctly has little to do with resolving the real issues of divorce.

Collaborative Divorce helps divorcing couples comprehensively address the problems that need to be settled and helps them devise creative solutions that really work.

Maintaining Strong Viewpoints without Becoming Adversarial

We know the conflicts and disputes that arise in divorce are powerful and can be terribly damaging if they get out of control.

People have big and significant differences and disputes to work out in divorce. Strong viewpoints collide with one another. Some people may try to prevent fights by avoiding the differences that exist, worried that if they express their viewpoints, blow ups are inevitable. The only choices may seem to be either minimizing differences or addressing them and ending up in huge battles.

Collaborative Divorce is committed to helping people settle significant disagreements without turning them into poisonous fights.

Staying Out of Court

The courts are overwhelmed by the sheer volume of divorces, and each case gets only the briefest review. People who are divorcing may fantasize that if only they get to court, the judge will rule in their favor. Or, just the opposite, they may imagine the judge will be totally against them. The process of going to court is unpredictable and confusing. When divorcing couples take unresolved disputes to court, they end up leaving the most personal and crucial decisions in the hands of busy strangers.

Collaborative Divorce is committed to helping couples responsibly resolve their big and small differences out of court. In Collaborative Divorce, people never have to face the trauma of going to court.

Planning a Healthy Future for the Children

Divorce is tough on children, and it's vital to pay attention to their special needs during and after divorce. Otherwise, the children get lost in the shuffle, caught in the cross fire and burdened by their parents' troubled relationship.

Children can be spared some of the worst pain and trauma of divorce if their parents actively focus on and communicate about the children's needs and how these needs can be provided for.

Collaborative Divorce ensures that children's needs are known and heard. Planning for a healthy future for the children is a priority that is held in mind every step of the way.

Seeing the Whole Picture

Communication and collaboration among professionals working together to help divorcing couples make it easier for couples to solve their problems.

Coordinated efforts bring help to the entire divorcing family; the perspective of each person is recognized and appreciated. Collaborative Divorce aims for solutions that are sound and healthy and contribute to the well-being of all family members.

Advocates of Collaborative Divorce believe when professionals work together to "see the whole elephant," conflict can be contained instead of running rampant,

the divorce process can be humane and the stage can be set for a civil and constructive post-divorce relationship between divorcing parents.

Understanding the Family's Hopes and Fears

Divorce fills people with hopes and fears. The fears are about all that they stand to lose, all that is unknown about the future and all that they believe is true about the damaging and difficult nature of divorce. Their hopes are about the other side of the coin: what they can imagine gaining, how they envision the future they want and how they hope to stay afloat and manage during a time of significant change.

Collaborative Divorce is a team approach in which the specialists understand and respect the hopes and fears of divorcing couples. Collaborative Divorce is committed to helping these couples make it through divorce and into the future so they can face their fears and realize their dreams.

8 Collaborative Divorce: A Team Approach

How Does the Collaborative Divorce Team Work?

The Collaborative Divorce team consists of divorce counselors, child counselors, financial counselors and attorneys. These professionals work together to help divorcing couples address the issues they face in constructive, coordinated and effective ways.

The divorce counselors help divorcing couples sort out and understand feelings, review their situations and clarify and prioritize their needs. They coach couples in structured and constructive communications. The divorce counselors coordinate the Collaborative Divorce team effort.

The child counselors meet with the children and provide them an opportunity to share their stories about the changes in the family and discuss questions and concerns they may have about these changes. The child counselor is also available to meet with parents to help them in their decision making about the children.

The financial counselor meets with a divorcing couple (1) to help them manage any immediate and/or temporary financial crises or misunderstandings, (2) to begin discussions about how the financial pie is to be divided, (3) to help them with the budgetary aspects of divorce and (4) to aid them in the process of organizing and disclosing the necessary financial information.

The collaborative law attorneys provide legal representation to individuals in the divorce process but do so in a framework of working collaboratively rather than adversarially. They agree to help their clients consider solutions to divorce-related problems that are responsive to and respectful of the needs and concerns of both husband and wife. Collaborative Divorce attorneys provide legal representation to their clients in the spirit of seeking solutions in which both sides win, rather than solutions that end in fights and result in court battles.

The Collaborative Divorce Agreement is a signed agreement in which a couple and the team of divorce specialists agree about the basic rules that will guide the Collaborative Divorce process.

Where Do People Start?

Our experience is that divorcing couples begin the process with their most pressing need. Some people want to meet with a collaborative law attorney first to get information about the legal aspects of divorce. Others feel so overwhelmed by the emotional stress of the situation (anger, hurt, despair, shock) that they need to talk with a counselor on their own before anything else is possible. Some couples begin by meeting together with divorce counselors to do some initial exploration and sorting out of differences. Where worries about money matters loom heavily, meeting with a financial counselor is the first step.

People begin wherever they feel they need the most immediate help. Each unique situation determines the strategy and the order of dealing with all the aspects of the divorce.

Sometimes both partners aren't ready to start the process at the same time. For example, the wife may begin on her own and the husband may join later on. In situations where only one person is interested in the Collaborative Divorce approach, we work with that person alone. We believe that even if only one of the partners is committed to handling the divorce process using the principles of collaboration, the process is much less likely to get out of control.

The next five chapters describe the Collaborative Divorce process and detail the role of each specialist in helping divorcing couples make their way through the divorce process. These next chapters also describe how each part of the Collaborative Divorce process benefits families facing divorce.

9 *The Divorce Counselors*

The scariest part of divorce may be the roller coaster ride of emotions. When facing divorce, people want to stay in control of their lives. They want to get a handle on their runaway emotions.

When everything is "up for grabs" and everything is bound to change, people need to review their priorities and decide what matters most. However, the roller coaster ride of complicated feelings and thoughts interferes with divorcing couples' problem-solving and decision-making abilities. They can't effectively "do business" with one

another if they are flooded with emotions and/or unable to think clearly.

In the Collaborative Divorce model, clients meet with divorce counselors to get some initial help and support in handling the roller coaster of complicated feelings and thoughts. Each adult typically has his or her own counselor, usually of the same sex. On occasion, a single counselor will see both adults individually if a situation seems to call for it.

Because divorce is such a personal matter, approaching a counselor during the stressful time of divorce is sometimes difficult. Having a divorce counselor or coach, however, gives each person a unique opportunity to voice concerns and sort out the mix of emotions that accompany divorce. A trained counselor can help

address divorce fears such as, How can I get my point across when I'm so nervous I can't think straight? How will I be able to make good decisions when I am so filled with anger? We could never agree on anything in our marriage, won't divorce make the problem worse?

Four-Way Meetings

The initial meetings with a counselor help a person get organized and prepared to meet and talk with his or her spouse. When they feel ready, the divorcing couple meet accompanied by their counselors. In four-way meetings, the counselors help the divorcing couple bring up their concerns. Important feelings, thoughts and issues are aired and discussed by the couple, and with the help of the counselors, the couple work to avoid pushing each other's "hot buttons." These four-way meetings can establish the groundwork for a civil working relationship that helps the couple get through the divorce process more easily.

During this period, the divorcing couple may, if needed, learn effective conflict-resolution skills that help them

build their confidence in addressing tough problems. Problems that may have seemed insurmountable in the beginning of the process can be tackled successfully with new skills in place and with support and encouragement.

Feedback from the Child Counselor

A child counselor provides feedback and information about the children from an objective, professional point of view. The counselor helps parents appreciate how the changes in the family are perceived by the children and how the children are managing these changes. The child counselor helps parents understand and address the needs of each child. During the four-way meeting, this feedback, along with general information about the chil-dren's development, helps parents make plans and agreements that are appropriate for their children.

Family Meetings

The entire family—children and parents—may meet with the counselors. In family meetings, counselors ensure that each family member receives the support he or she needs to be able to share feelings and concerns about the changes in the family. During these sessions, the counselors both support and facilitate a process wherein each person in the family can share his or her point of view about the divorce and be heard by the others. Better communication between family members makes problem solving more effective and more satisfying.

Benefits of the Collaborative Divorce Process

By participating in the Collaborative Divorce process, divorcing adults can move ahead with the business of divorce, knowing that their hopes and fears about the process have been heard and respected. When people are being heard and respected, they are better able to focus clearly on the decisions at hand. In addition, they gain a framework for communication that helps them effectively tackle the problems divorce brings as well as the challenges they face after divorce.

"I was as scared as I've ever been when John and I met for the first time with our divorce counselors. Somehow I envisioned a meeting where John would convince everyone to see things his way. He is so convincing, and I am usually the shy one. But it didn't happen that way. For the first time I can remember, I actually said what I was thinking. John truly listened and with our counselors' support, we accomplished a "first"—an agreement we can both live with.

John's story: "Mary never tells me what she wants. She just gets angry when she doesn't get it. I thought our divorce would be like that as well. My divorce counselor helped me see that I wouldn't lose anything by listening, and it helped me get clarity. It turned out we weren't as far apart as I feared. I'm relieved to find out that we can get through this without destroying each other."

10 *The Child Counselors*

Children and Divorce

In the midst of the many changes and stresses that adults juggle during divorce, what happens to the children? Surrounded by all the adult activity relating to divorce, children are like sponges soaking up information, friction and anxiety. Just as there's a lot going on for the adults, the children have a lot to deal with, too.

Children try to make sense of what is happening. Why are Mom and Dad splitting up? Often, children worry that they may be partly to blame. They need reassurance, they need information, and they need the opportunity to express their feelings.

What Children Tell Counselors

Joel, age five: "If Mommy leaves Daddy, will Mommy leave me?"

Mary, age six: "I have been thinking . . . I'd better go to Grandma's house 'cuz Dad left and Mom's mad and going to leave too. I think Grandma will take me."

Paul, age seven: "Will we be able to keep the dog?"

Kristen, age ten: "I feel like this is the worst year of my life. Everything's ruined."

Jenny, age thirteen: "I think everyone at school is going to ask questions and I don't want anyone to know."

Divorce means change—usually lots of change. When many changes are being discussed or begin to happen, the biggest question in children's minds is, What about *me*? What's going to happen to *me*? Some children ask these questions very directly. Some show their concerns and worries in how they behave. Others worry their questions will only add to their parents' distress, so they keep their questions, thoughts and feelings to themselves. Regardless, What about *me*? is a question that weighs heavily on the mind of any child whose parents are divorcing.

What About Me?

When their moms and dads decide to divorce, children want to know what's happening and how it will affect them. Divorce itself is a huge and unwelcome surprise. Children don't want any more surprises.

Children want to know what to expect and who they can count on. They want to feel assured and confident that their parents can handle their own adult problems and will continue to handle the job of being parents as well.

Children want to feel good about their families. They want to feel that the future holds something to look forward to and that it will not be ruined by divorce. They want to be able to protest and complain about the changes in the family and have those sentiments understood and respected.

Children want to keep connections with both Mom and Dad. They want to be reassured that they can count on these connections and that their parents will work out the details in a way that doesn't burden the children or ask them to choose sides.

They want to know that the family matters and that even though a divorce is a sad family event, family life continues to be important and valued. They want to be able to count on their parents to show them a positive view of the future.

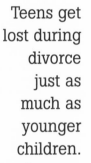

Teens get lost during divorce just as much as younger children. They need someone outside the family to listen to them and help them know what to expect. Children who are away at college when their parents divorce can be devastated, feeling they have no home base any more. Just because older children look like they can take care of themselves and enjoy their independence doesn't mean they don't object to the changes that divorce brings. Even the most self-reliant teen looks at his or her parents' divorce and wonders, What about me?

"I don't know what this divorce means for me. I was planning to go away to college, but I think Mom needs me now. I'm glad to have someone to talk to about this. I hate to upset Mom by talking about what I want. I haven't seen Dad since he left; I got a letter, but that's all."

"I'm sick of hearing about how wrong Mom is, but I don't know what to say to Dad to shut him up. I get mad at both of them when they talk about each other."

"Will Dad still come see my baseball games?"

"How am I going to decide who to ask to the school play I'm in next month?"

What the Child Counselor Does

In Collaborative Divorce, a child counselor meets with children to give them an opportunity to discuss what's changing in their family and to bring to light their most important questions and concerns about these changes.

Children of divorcing couples meet with a Collaborative Divorce child counselor so that the children's points of view about the changes in the family get heard and recognized.

The child counselor provides a comfortable place for children to tell the important story about how their family is changing. Children can explore some of the thoughts, feelings, questions, worries and speculations they might have about why these changes have happened and why their parents are divorcing. In addition, they have a chance to offer their own ideas about how to minimize the disruption to their lives.

HOW THE CHILD COUNSELOR HELPS THE CHILDREN

The child counselor talks with the children about divorce in a way that they understand and eases painful feelings of shame and isolation. Meeting with a child counselor comforts the children by communicating to them that they are important and that their point of view is valued. It provides the children with a place to voice concerns they've been reluctant or afraid to bring up with their parents. The counselor can also act as a helper or advocate in communications with the parents if the children feel their parents are not tuned in to their concerns, needs or preferences.

HOW THE CHILD COUNSELOR HELPS THE PARENTS

The Collaborative Divorce child counselor helps parents by offering assurance that their children's points of view are considered with care and compassion. In addition, the counselor pro-

vides expert advice on how to best help children through the tough time of divorce. Lastly, parents get help developing practical and comprehensive co-parenting plans that are based on the specific needs of each child.

11 Formulating Co-Parenting Agreements for the Post-Divorce Years

Planning for the Future: What Do the Children Need?

Information from the child counselor helps parents cope with their immediate concerns about the children during divorce. Parents gain understanding about the stresses their children undergo, and they increase their confidence in handling problems that arise. The Collaborative Divorce child counselor also helps parents plan for the future.

Most often, both parents want to be actively involved in their children's lives after the divorce. This requires developing a plan both parents can agree upon that really works for their children.

The Co-Parenting Plan

A co-parenting plan or child custody arrangement is the set of agreements that divorcing parents make about the legal responsibilities of each parent and the practical arrangements for taking care of the children after the divorce. Putting together a good co-parenting plan requires a lot from divorcing couples. Although they are in the midst of untangling most of the significant emotional, financial and legal linkages of marriage, the object of a co-parenting plan is to help a couple work together as parents in the present and into the future as the children grow. Sharing responsibility for the children is one bond that continues after divorce. Parents continue to have a common interest in the well-being and care of their children even though they have severed ties as a married couple.

"Brian doesn't want to take tennis lessons; he wants to do gymnastics. My wife thinks I'm the one pushing gymnastics, but I'm not. I don't care what sport Brian plays, as long as he's happy."

"We both want to stay involved with our daughter's soccer team. I'm not sure how we're going to work this out, but I do know she wants both of us to come to her games."

DEVELOPING A CO-PARENTING PLAN

In order to develop a co-parenting plan, parents need to take a careful look at each of their children. What are the nature and temperament of each child? What are the children's ages and what are the special challenges of growing up that each one faces? How do they deal with upset and change? What helps them adjust to change? What are their questions and concerns about the divorce?

The way a three-year-old responds to divorce is quite different from the way a fifteen-year-old handles it. Arrangements that are right for one may not work for the other. Ways of helping each of them with the adjustments to divorce may differ. Children are individuals; in making decisions about their lives, their unique and specific circumstances must be appreciated. A co-parenting plan is a living document that should be tailor-made and modified with the changing needs of each child.

After taking stock of each child and his or her needs, parents can then begin to decide what their co-parenting agreement should include. How can the plan ensure that the children get the care they need? Where will the children live? Will they live mostly with one parent or will they split their time more or less evenly between Mom's house and Dad's house? What are the plans for vacations, holidays and birthdays? How do the parents want to coordinate their time and involvement in the children's lives and activities like sports, scout activities and music lessons? What's the plan for emergencies?

"I really feel uncomfortable around my ex. I hate bumping into her, especially at one of Jake's baseball games. After a while, we decided the best way to deal with the problem is for each of us to go to half the games this season. I've got the evens; she's got the odds. Maybe it will be better next year and we won't have to make such a big deal about it. But for now, this works okay. I know it's a relief to Jake. He doesn't have to worry that his mom and I are going to get into a fight in the parking lot after his games."

"I want the kids to see their dad a lot, but it's tricky to figure out a system that will work for both kids. Sam's thirteen and he wants to spend half his time at his dad's house. This makes sense to me, but the baby's only fourteen months old. He's never even spent one night away from me!"

A plan that works is made for the current situation but looks beyond it as well. It anticipates the unseen changes that the future holds. While it's possible that a good plan may provide all the guidelines the divorced parents will ever need, more often than not, life serves up surprises that need to be taken into account.

Children's needs change as they get older, but that's not all that changes. Families change, too. A parent's remarriage, the challenges facing stepfamilies, the arrival of a new baby and geographical moves are among the many family changes that can be unsettling to the children. No matter how good the initial agreements are, they most likely will need to be updated occasionally. The co-parenting plan needs to be reviewed and revised when changes occur that make the plan no longer viable, workable or optimal. A good co-parenting plan includes a method for dealing with change and specifies how parents will work out disputes or disagreements that arise in the future.

BENEFITS OF A CO-PARENTING PLAN

Collaborative Divorce helps parents stop and take a careful look at what's happening with each of their children. In doing so, parents make sure the children don't get lost in the shuffle.

Disagreements and disputes about planning for the children are common during divorce. Even parents who are not divorced disagree on various aspects of parenting, so it's no surprise to find divorcing couples at odds. Collaborative Divorce helps parents air, discuss, argue and resolve big and small disagreements. Using constructive problem solving, parents create a plan for coordinated parenting and they avoid an ongoing tug of war over the children.

"The plan we had for Andy when he started preschool was great at first, but then I changed jobs and needed to work longer hours. We've had to figure out a new arrangement, and so far, it's working. But we may need to change it again when Andy starts first grade."

"I was really relieved that we could work out a way for both of us to be at Rachel's birthday party. I was worried I'd have to miss it."

Collaborative Divorce also helps parents develop an understanding of how plans will be reviewed and revised later when changes in the children's lives or in the family call for updating existing plans.

"I'm getting married again soon, and I'm really anxious about how my ex-wife is going to react."

"I'd like to get married again next summer, but my ex-husband is going to be very upset about it. I don't want anyone to take his place with the

kids, but that's what he thinks will happen. I think he's going to make it rough on the kids, and this really makes me sad; I'd like them to get a chance to enjoy the wedding."

Parenting is a treasured part of adult life. At the time of divorce, worries surface about how to manage the demands of parenting alone. Collaborative Divorce helps people look forward to enjoying the experiences of being parents.

Being able to coordinate parenting responsibilities so that the children do not bear the burden of the adults' disputes is one of the most meaningful and valuable gifts divorcing parents can give to their children. Then the children get the best of both parents. Collaborative Divorce helps parents find a way to give this gift.

The goal of Collabora-
tive Divorce is to help
divorcing couples
do the best they
can for their chil-
dren at the time of
divorce and in the
future.

12 *The Financial Counselors*

One of the biggest questions that surfaces in divorce is, How will we divide up what we own? People worry about how the financial pie will be divided, whether or not there will be enough money to go around, who will get what and what the financial picture will look like in the future.

Coming up with answers to these questions requires that lots of information be gathered, organized and considered. In the midst of divorce, financial pressures can feel overwhelming and impossible to cope with. People worry about the long-term financial outcomes, and they also face trying to stay afloat while the divorce is being negotiated.

How the Financial Counselor Helps

People who are divorcing save time and money when they work collaboratively with a financial counselor, rather than duplicating one another's efforts. The financial counselor helps sort out and make sense of the family finances. Divorcing couples get help with handling immediate dilemmas, anticipating the financial responsibilities they face as parents and organizing their finances so that they can negotiate fair financial settlements. Depending on their preferences, divorcing couples meet jointly or separately with the financial counselor throughout this process.

IMMEDIATE FINANCIAL CONCERNS

During divorce, anxiety about money can run high. Some divorcing couples may need to agree on temporary monetary arrangements right away. An impartial and realistic look at income and budgets helps the divorcing couple figure out how to "divide the pie" so that everyone has enough money to live on in the short run. Establishing a basic understanding about how the family's finances will be protected during the divorce helps relieve the stress and makes it easier to talk about long-term arrangements.

FINANCIAL RESPONSIBILITIES AND THE CHILDREN

The financial counselor helps divorcing couples consider how they will handle the financial responsibilities of raising the children. The immediate needs of the children are apparent, but it takes some forethought to anticipate their future needs.

The financial support children need at a young age is different from what they require later on. When parents work together from the beginning to anticipate the financial requirements of raising the children, they can prepare themselves for the inevitable changes in their children's needs.

While all future financial issues can't be anticipated or decided upon early in the divorce process, ground rules for making financial decisions about the children can be set up. These ground rules are helpful and important because they can prevent misunderstandings and dis- agreements about the parents' financial responsibilities. They also give parents a way to deal with any future dis- putes that may arise.

PREPARING TO NEGOTIATE THE FINAL SETTLEMENT

In Collaborative Divorce, the financial counselor helps couples organize their essential financial information and consider possible choices for dividing community or marital property. Until all the facts and figures are "on the table," it is impossible even to begin negotiations. The financial counselor helps clarify all of the financial issues so that both husband and wife fully understand their financial situation.

"I feel so much better knowing that I am not going to be left with nothing. I was amazed that we had so much, and Bill seemed so reasonable when we talked. I was surprised we could even

talk about this. He has always been so tight with money."

———

Divorcing couples take the information that the financial counselor has helped them organize to their attorneys, who then help them negotiate a fair, long-term settlement. When divorcing couples go to their attorneys with their money matters straightened out, their information documented for the legal process and a basic understanding of the whole picture, the attorneys can focus effectively and efficiently on finalizing a settlement. This procedure makes the best use of the attorneys' time, and it saves the divorcing couple time and money as well.

Benefits of Working with the Financial Counselor

Working with the financial counselor minimizes conflicts. Facts about finances are separated from the emotions that may cloud the situation. People are able to move the process forward at a pace that is comfortable. This reduces the worry that they might get "railroaded" into making a decision before they are fully informed. Careful and thorough clarification of all issues reduces the fear and anxiety that surround discussions about fair property settlement.

"I thought the house was worth a lot until the counselor explained that we also owe a lot on it. It was a shock because I thought I would keep the house, but now I understand why I have to move into a place that fits in my budget."

13 The Role of the Attorneys

In Collaborative Divorce the attorneys practice collaborative law. Therefore, we first need to explain the concept of collaborative law.

The Practice of Collaborative Law

Collaborative law is a new and emerging framework used for negotiating formal legal agreements. The goal of collaborative law is to resolve legal differences in a just and equitable way without going to court, arguing the facts and the law, or giving the decision-making power to a judge. When people with legal problems, such as divorce, decide to use collaborative law, they and their attorneys negotiate agreements that become court orders.

In collaborative law, attorneys represent the interests and points of view of their individual clients, but they do so guided by the principle of settling disputes through communication and negotiation. This means the desired result is a win–win outcome instead of the win–lose outcome inherent in the traditional competitive and adversarial framework.

Using the principles of collaborative law, attorneys and their clients agree to work toward a thorough understanding and consideration of the interests and perspectives of both parties. Disagreements that are identified are carefully and respectfully explored. Both sides create settlement proposals that are refined through negotiation so that they meet the fundamental needs of both parties.

Collaborative law is a welcome alternative to the traditional combative approach of resolving legal disputes.

The Attorney's Role In Collaborative Law

While the attorney remains an advisor about legal issues to his or her client, the attorney and client work together to develop creative solutions that meet the interests of both spouses. In collaborative law, solving problems through negotiation is viewed as being in the best interests of both sides. The attorney acts as a legal counselor for the client—an expert advisor with experience and training in legal matters.

Collaborative attorneys, along with the individuals they represent, work as members of a settlement team, not as adversaries. Existing or developing disputes and disagreements are approached as problems to be solved, and the attorneys work in a cooperative way to help create solutions that are acceptable to both sides.

 Collaborative attorneys are concerned about the process as well as the outcome of legal proceedings. They know how damaging—financially and emotionally—legal battles can become. In divorce, the cost to families, and particularly to children, is huge when differences escalate and result in legal battles.

Experienced negotiators know that agreements that are mutually acceptable to both sides of a dispute are more likely to be kept than decisions made by judges, especially in divorce cases.

"I didn't know anything about collaborative law . . . my husband's attorney suggested it. My husband liked it because he figured it would be less expensive. I went along with it because I knew I'd have my own advocate, which I really needed. I was afraid that if we chose mediation, I'd get bowled over. I was scared to negotiate with my husband."

"I knew she was afraid of lawyers and that her brother was telling her to get a 'shark' to protect herself. I was pretty sure it was going to get ugly, so when I approached her about using collaborative attorneys, I was surprised she agreed. I

guess we'd each made the other out to be the 'bad guy,' and I'm really relieved it didn't turn into a big fight."

The Collaborative Law Attorney and the Collaborative Divorce Process

Attorneys practicing collaborative law are key members of the Collaborative Divorce team. In their commitment to work collaboratively on behalf of their clients, they seek to change the divorce system itself, avoiding the disaster stories that easily develop when the divorce turns into a legal battle.

Just like any other attorney, Collaborative Divorce attorneys help their clients understand the law. The Collaborative Divorce attorneys also help their clients carefully evaluate their options so that they not only know what they have "the right to do" but also thoughtfully consider what is "right to do."

Clear and understandable explanations about the law are important, but they're not enough. Clients also want common-sense help analyzing the short- and long-term effects of the options they have available. Collaborative Divorce attorneys help people fully understand their legal choices and keep control of their lives during the divorce process.

How Collaborative Attorneys Work with Other Professionals

All members of the Collaborative Divorce team help the clients prepare for their negotiations with the attorneys. The divorcing individuals come to the negotiating table with strengthened abilities to cope with their feelings and communicate effectively. They have prioritized their needs and concerns and have had an opportunity to thoughtfully consider the current and future needs of their children. They have begun to organize their finances and begun to consider the range of options available to them in dividing property and arranging custody. They come to the negotiating table well-organized and confident that their perspectives and their concerns will be thoroughly and accurately represented.

How Does the Collaborative Divorce Attorney Work?

In the Collaborative Divorce model, divorcing individuals and their attorneys enter into negotiations by signing an agreement that specifies the ground rules they've set and accepted for discussing their issues. Clients meet privately with their respective attorneys. Frequently, some problems need immediate solutions, such as temporary arrangements for payment of bills, use of cars and support. The attorneys and their clients concentrate on those issues first. When both parties feel prepared and ready for direct negotiations, they and their attorneys meet together in four-way meetings and develop acceptable temporary solutions. These solutions are presented to the court in writing (no appearance in court is necessary) and become court orders.

Individual Meetings with Attorneys

Once the agreement to work collaboratively is made, attorneys and clients then begin the normal process of addressing legal concerns. In prior conversations with divorce counselors, and with child and financial counselors, divorcing couples have already identified important individual perspectives and prioritized concerns and issues. Collaborative Divorce attorneys help their clients develop and discuss the legal aspects of their divorce-related concerns. In some cases, other members of the Collaborative Divorce team may meet with the attorney and client to contribute to the discussion of some issues. Collaborative Divorce attorneys add the legal information and advice needed to develop thoughtful and realistic proposals.

Clients may also get help anticipating and preparing for the four-way negotiation process that follows individual meetings. The attorneys make sure their clients have had ample time to consider fully the situation and their own individual needs, wishes and concerns before four-way meetings are initiated.

"I liked the idea of having my own attorney. I talked with her a lot at the beginning to help me decide what I really wanted, what my real positions were and just to get informed. It helped to

know she'd speak for me when I needed her to do so. At first, she did most of the talking for me, but then I started understanding more about the process. She coached me and helped me understand what was realistic to expect."

"I knew the custody plan was going to be our big snag. What surprised me was how we were able to work out something that was good for the kids and acceptable to us too. I thought the lawyers would just tell us what to do, but they helped us figure out some decent possibilities and then we talked about them quite a bit. Finally, the best plan just seemed to surface."

FOUR-WAY MEETINGS

Four-way meetings are held when both clients are fully ready to meet and negotiate together. These meetings, which include both attorneys and both clients, focus on discovering common ground, identifying problems, clarifying points of view, exchanging necessary information and considering and negotiating agreements. The clients are an integral part of this process, and the attorneys serve as active advocates for their clients' perspectives as well as for the collaborative process. If helpful or necessary, other Collaborative Divorce team members can join these meetings.

Thorough disclosure of all pertinent financial information is part of the process. Both sides are fully informed about all information that is relevant to the issues being decided. Attorneys ensure that the information, perspective and understanding that their clients have gained from conversations with the divorce counselors, and with the child counselor and the financial counselor, are incorporated into any final proposals and agreements.

> *"When it was over, I felt it was a win-win situation. I left with my dignity; I think we both did, which was kind of a surprise. I felt the settlement was very fair. Even the four-way meeting turned out to be positive. I actually felt a lot better about myself by the end of the whole process, like I'd had a 'crash course' in life and survived."*

Collaborative attorneys and their clients carefully evaluate proposed agreements to ensure that they are compatible with the clients' goals and wishes. All decisions must be acceptable to both spouses.

The collaborative effort does not stop when disputes become complicated; collaborative law attorneys are dedicated to solving thorny issues in a nonadversarial way. If issues heat up or the clients become discouraged, the attorneys may suggest a break, but they don't give up; they persist in working toward agreements that are acceptable to both sides. This is a constructive rather than destructive process. The members of the Collaborative Divorce team remain available as additional problem solvers and can be called in as needed.

The anticipated outcome of meetings with Collaborative Divorce attorneys is a collaboratively negotiated divorce agreement. The agreements necessary to formally end the marriage are put into writing. Successful agreements are viewed by both sides as fair; they serve the divorcing couple and their children well after the divorce.

When final agreements are reached, the attorneys put them into a written contract, which is clearly understood and signed by both parties. Then the attorneys submit the agreement to the court for the judge's signature; no court appearances are necessary. The divorce then becomes final.

Benefits of Working with a Collaborative Divorce Attorney

Collaborative Divorce attorneys help their clients clarify personal perspectives, concerns and interests. The commitment to solving problems and developing agreements in a collaborative and constructive manner is of immense value to the clients: the goal of this approach is to keep people out of court. Collaborative Divorce helps people effectively complete the divorce process without enduring the truly awful experience of an escalating and ugly legal battle.

In the Collaborative Divorce model, attorneys help divorcing couples

- keep the lid on the tensions that exist and avoid legal escalations;

- develop solutions that really work for both sides;

- take responsibility for and maintain control of the important issues involved in divorce;

- protect themselves and their children from unnecessary stress and pain during and after divorce;

- minimize their legal expenses;

- feel respected and "heard" in the divorce process.

14 Collaborative Divorce: The Ripple Effect of Divorce

Reading a dramatic story of a divorce among the "rich and famous" or a gut-wrenching account of an exceptionally horrific divorce may cause us to feel outraged or saddened or disgusted. We can comfort ourselves by thinking such events happen far away to people unlike ourselves. But we cannot isolate ourselves from divorce. Close to half of those who marry will eventually divorce.

Divorce is a part of our culture, and divorces of every kind—rough and conflict-ridden, sad and painful, mutually agreed upon—are happening in every neighborhood, every community, every part of the country. Divorce can happen in any kind of marriage: in ones where a breakup was predicted and in ones that looked idyllic to the outside world.

The truth is, every divorce has a lasting effect. All family members carry with them the experience of how they and their family negotiated the rough waters of divorce.

Every divorce has a ripple effect. When a divorce is handled in a combative, hostile way, its negative effects extend out beyond the members of the immediate family. The ripple effects of destructive divorces leave in their wake many strained relationships and estrangements. Children become cut off from grandparents, holidays become a source of conflict and anxiety, and family members feel that they have failed or have permanently conflicting loyalties. Children are deprived of opportunities and economic support when either parent withholds financial resources.

The ripple effects of destructive divorces go well beyond the lives of even the extended family. When divorce is allowed to undermine the capability of parents to provide their children with the attention and love they need or when children suffer significant losses of self-esteem and emotional or economic well-being, the losses extend out into the wider community. When we let our children down in this way, they lose, and the rest of us—the larger community—lose as well. With a million children exposed to their parents' divorces every year, the stakes are high—high for each and every one of those children and for our society as a whole.

The Ripple Effect of Collaborative Divorce

Collaborative Divorces produce ripple effects that are positive and enriching. When divorcing couples undertake the very difficult task of untangling the ties that bind in a constructive and respectful way, the future they make possible for themselves and their children is quite different than when more traditional divorce processes are followed.

The ripple effect of a Collaborative Divorce makes it possible for family members to preserve and protect valued connections with one another despite the end of a marriage. Children are relieved of the pressure to choose between their parents and instead have easy access to each parent. Children know that their parents, though no longer a couple in marriage, can and do provide for their emotional and financial needs in a coordinated way.

The Vision of Collaborative Divorce

Having worked with so many divorcing families and having witnessed the ripples that extend out from these divorces, we are firm in our convictions and clear in our vision about the importance of providing divorcing couples and families with the help they need to find a constructive path through the divorce process. We are committed to addressing the problems of divorce and the problems of the current system in a way that will provide true and reliable help for divorcing couples.

Collaborative Divorce offers a powerful alternative model for viewing and managing the process of divorce. We hope the message in this book opens the door to the discussion, consideration and implementation of these new ideas and perspectives.

APPENDIX I

Commonly Asked Questions about Collaborative Divorce

This appendix presents the answers to the most commonly asked questions about Collaborative Divorce.

- *What kinds of problems are resolved by the Collaborative Divorce process?*

  The process is comprehensive and helps clients find solutions to all of the problems relating to divorce—emotional, financial and legal. It can't address long-standing emotional problems, and it can't produce a budget that exceeds the income.

- *Will it cost more to involve all these professionals?*
  The cost depends on the complexity of the divorce case, the number of children involved and the level of hostility between the parties. What Collaborative

Divorce does is contain the conflict and work toward a solution for the whole divorce problem. It reduces the time spent with attorneys carrying on a conflict that is about feelings, not facts. Most importantly, you retain control of your own life. You make the decisions, not a judge. The process is private and confidential. You reduce future hostility that may build up into a costly court battle. You save the high cost of going to court. In the end you and your former spouse are much more likely to keep the agreements you have carefully made.

- *Do we have to use all the team members?*
  Childless couples with short-term relationships may use only some of the team members. However, our experience is that each team member can be very helpful. When children are involved, the relationship between the couple must continue at least until the children are grown. Our process facilitates this relationship.

- *What are the advantages of having a financial counselor?*
  The financial counselor helps you deal with all the practical issues of your divorce and collect all the financial information you need to fill out your divorce papers. You need this same information to fairly divide the assets and debts, determine support and plan future household budgets. The financial counselor gives both parties information, discusses options and helps the couple understand

what they need to know to negotiate the financial decisions.

- *How is collaborative law different from mediation?*
  One mediator remains neutral and assists both parties in working out their agreement; but in collaborative law, both parties have attorneys to help and support each of them in creating a solution.

- *My spouse is so argumentative, how could we possibly go through a Collaborative Divorce?*
  The divorce counselors, financial counselor, child counselor and attorneys are all trained to help clients gain the perspective necessary to use constructive communication and find constructive solutions to differences.

- *What happens if the process doesn't seem to work for us?*
  You can withdraw from the process at any time and pursue other alternatives. However, we encourage our clients to persevere because the alternatives usually do not work as well as the Collaborative Divorce process.

- *Does the team make decisions if we can't?*
  Once the parties begin to reach agreement on some issues, they generally feel they can make agreements on the remaining issues. We find that when the team works together, creative ways are found to take care of seemingly unresolvable issues between couples. Sometimes introducing new ideas through a consultant or joint expert is helpful. If all else fails,

an independent judge and voluntary settlement conferences are possible solutions.

- *If my wife already has an attorney and I want to use this process, how can I work this out?*
  We have found that working with only one party is still very beneficial because even if one person is able to maintain a collaborative approach, the whole process goes more smoothly. If only one person is fighting, it is more difficult to have a war.

- *Is Collaborative Divorce only for married couples?*
  Collaborative Divorce also helps couples who are not married but have children, as well as same-sex couples who face the end of long-term relationships and share many things including children.

- *How will my legal interests be protected if I choose Collaborative Divorce?*
  Each client is represented by a collaborative law attorney to safeguard that client's legal interest.

- *Will a judge accept our agreement?*
  Judges accept divorcing spouses' written agreements. Judges generally will not accept agreements that are obviously unfair or not permitted under state law. For example, divorcing parents may not waive their children's right to support. Experienced Collaborative Divorce attorneys draft written agreements that will pass judicial review.

- *Who pays the expenses?*
  Normally, the expenses of a divorce are shared by both parties.

Training to Develop a Collaborative Divorce Group in Your Area

The Collaborative Divorce group offers the following training in the Collaborative Divorce process:

1. Introduction:

    Day-long integrated program. Overview of the Collaborative Divorce integrated program

2. Training Weekend I:

    The three parts of the Collaborative Divorce process: emotional, financial and legal and their integration.

    Training Weekend II:

    Intensive training for each of the three professions. Simulated cases working with supervision from the Collaborative Divorce staff.

3. Consultation on the formation of new Collaborative Divorce groups.

Training is open to

- Licensed mental health professionals with training in family therapy.

- Attorneys with a family law specialty.

- Accounting professionals such as financial managers, CPAs, real estate investors, financial planners and business managers who have the skills and sensitivity to work with people facing challenging and difficult life transitions.

If you wish more information, please copy this page and mail or fax it to us.

Name: _____

Title: _____

Organization: _____

Address: _____

City: _____ State: _____ ZIP: _____

Phone: _____ Fax: _____

E-mail: _____

Collaborative Divorce
P.O. Box 175
Orinda, CA 94563
Tel: 510-253-0700
Fax: 510-254-5985
Website: www.collaborativedivorce.com

About the Authors

Karen Fagerstrom, Ph.D., is a licensed psychologist who has specialized in the areas of marriage, family and divorce. After receiving post-doctoral training, she served as a staff psychologist at the Center for the Family in Transition in Corte Madera, California. Currently, Dr. Fagerstrom has a private practice in Berkeley, California, and is affiliated as a divorce counselor with Collaborative Divorce in Contra Costa County and as a senior staff member with the Bay Area Family in Transition Associates in Marin and Alameda Counties. In addition to her clinical work, she served as a research associate in a study on good marriages and is an adjunct faculty member at the California School for Professional Psychology in Alameda, California.

Milton Kalish, L.C.S.W., has eighteen years of clinical experience helping children and their families. He is a divorce and child counselor with Collaborative Divorce. He is a member of the Society for Clinical Social Work and the National Association of Social Workers. Formerly a preschool teacher, Mr. Kalish received his master's degree from Smith College School of Social Work and holds certificates from the Psychotherapy Institute and the Eye Movement Desensitization Reprocessing Institute.

A. Rodney Nurse, Ph.D., Co-director of Collaborative Divorce East Bay, is a diplomate in clinical psychology. He practices family, clinical and forensic psychology in Orinda, California, and is trained in Eye Movement Desensitization Reprocessing. Dr. Nurse is a fellow of the Society for Personality Assessment and chairs the Task Force on Forensic Issues for the Division of Family Psychology of the American Psychological Association and the Contra Costa County Psychological Association's Task Force on Guidelines for Custody Evaluations. Dr. Nurse is a member of the Association of Family Conciliation Courts and an affiliate member of the Contra Costa Bar Association. An author of various papers and book chapters, Dr. Nurse is writing *Psychological Testing with Families*, to be published by Wiley Press.

Nancy J. Ross, L.C.S.W., is the South Bay director of Collaborative Divorce and director of Bauer, Shepherd and Ross, a psychotherapy practice in Cupertino, California. She is a diplomate in clinical social work. She is a member of Management Consultants and serves on the ethics committee for the Employee Assistance Program Association. She is a lecturer on the clinical faculty of Stanford University, is a personal performance coach and consultant and is trained in Eye Movement Desensitization Reprocessing.

Peggy Thompson, Ph.D., is director of Collaborative Divorce East Bay in Orinda, California. She has been a licensed family psychologist for twenty years, specializing in treating children and families. For the last six years she has been intensely involved in the divorce process as a custody evaluator, special master and high-conflict counselor. She completed a year-long post-doctoral training program in custody evaluation. She is a member of the American Psychological Association and the Association of Family Conciliation Courts. She is a facilitator with the Eye Movement Desensitization Reprocessing Institute.

Diana A. Wilde-Neuman is the financial counselor with Collaborative Divorce East Bay. She is founder of The DIVORCE RESOURCE in Orinda, California, and co-founder of the Family Stress Center in Concord, California. Ms. Wilde-Neuman is experienced as a corporate financial manager, real estate investor, educator, trainer and community leader and has received numerous awards of excellence for her work. She received a bachelor of arts in English from the University of California, where she also completed her graduate work. Diana has worked closely with Dr. Thompson to integrate the financial services she provides into the Collaborative Divorce model.

Thomas W. Wolfrum, J.D., has been an attorney for twenty-five years and has limited his practice to family law for the past fifteen years. He is certified by the State Bar of California as a family law specialist and is a fellow of the American Academy of Matrimonial Lawyers. He received awards for contributions to the community in the field of divorce. He has appeared on television speaking about family law issues and frequently serves as judge pro tem in family law cases. He is a graduate of Hastings College of Law. He is a recognized expert in family law through his work toward demystifying the divorce process for his clients.